NERJA

Text by José Manuel Real Pascual

Photographs, design, lay-out and printing, entirely created by the technical department of EDITORIAL ESCUDO DE ORO, S.A.

3rd Edition, January 1995

I.S.B.N. 84-378-1590-8

Dep. Legal B. 1424-1995

Editorial Escudo de Oro, S.A.

A lovely view of the Balcón de Europa.

Calahonda beach and cliffs. ▷

NERJA

The municipality of Nerja is situated in the easternmost part of Málaga province. To the west, it adjoins the municipalities of Torrox and Frigiliana, to the north with Cómpeta, to the east with Granada province (for the most part, the municipality of Almuñécar) and to the south with the Mediterranean Sea. It is, therefore, the easternmost zone of both the Costa del Sol and of the district of La Axarquía. The main route through Nerja is the N-340, which links it with Málaga, 52 kilometres away, and with the coast of Granada.

Nerja, with a population of 14,000, is the main tourist resort of the eastern stretch of the Costa del Sol and the second most important in La Axarquía, after Vélez-Málaga, 25 kilometres away.

One of the main attractions of Nerja is its coastline. Unlike the other zones of the Costa del Sol, here the mountains reach the shore, forming majestic cliffs between which nestle picturesque coves and beaches. As we travel eastwards, these cliffs become higher and more frequent. From the viewpoint known as the Balcón de Europa («Balcony of Europe»), going towards Torrox, we find the following beaches: Caletilla, Playa del Salón, Torrecilla and Playazo (two kilometres of sand). To the east, up to Granada province, we find: Calahonda, Chorrillo, Carabeo and Carabeíllo, Burriana, the beaches and coves of Maro, Alberguillas and Cantarriján. The beauty of these beaches and cliffs makes them ideal for campers and lovers of water sports alike. The local authorities have im-

The Balcón de Europa.

View of the Church of San Salvador from the Balcón de Europa.

posed a number of limitations on this zone in order to protect it from the impact of mass tourism. Nerja is situated on a plain surrounded by the rising peaks of the last foothills of the Sierra Almijara, including such impressive mountains as El Alto del Cielo, El Almendrón, La Cabeza del Caballo, La Atalaya, Lomas Llanas and Navachica. This last, at an altitude of 1,832 metres, adjoins Granada province.

The municipality contains a large number of springs forming rivers and streams. Indeed, Nerja must have had many waterways since the earliest times, for the name of the town during the Moorish occupation was Narixa, which means «abundant spring». To the west of the town the River Chillar reaches the sea, swollen by the

Higuerón and the Seco. To the east is the River Maro, formed by the Barranco de la Coladilla, and the River de la Miel. Nerja enjoys a Mediterranean climate, these benign conditions combining with a number of unique factors to bless the area with a splendid climate. The surrounding mountains protect Nerja from the cold north winds, whilst the influence of the sea makes for milder temperatures, both in summer and in winter.

These climatic conditions, combined with the abundance of water, have allowed a rich agricultural industry to grow up here, famed for over one thousand years. In ancient times, sub-tropical fruits such as sugar cane and the cherimoya were introduced to the area, and in modern times such exotic prod-

The Church of San Salvador.

The Town Hall. ▷

ucts as papayas, mangoes and avocadoes have been added to the list. Vegetables such as batatas are also grown here, as well as traditional Mediterranean products like grapes, almonds and olives.

Another important activity in the area is fishing, but the main source of income in Nerja is now tourism. The pleasant climate in the zone, the beauty of the coastline and such tourist attractions as the Nerja Cave combine with the friendliness and hospitality of the local people and the excellent facilities to provide the visitor with all the comfort and entertainment he or she could wish. The amenities have been installed with maximum respect for urban and environmental conditions, and have been adapted to traditional Andalusian town planning and environmental impact minimised. Due to its tourist industry, the population of Nerja rises to 45,000 in summer.

Nerja offers a huge number of hotels of all categories and sizes, as well as bars, cafés and restaurants, from the typical Andalusian bodega to establishments serving the best in international cuisine, not forgetting the *chiringuito*, a tiny restaurant by the seaside specialising in fried fish and other typical Malagan dishes.

The area also has its Parador (national hotel), situated on a privileged site on the coast overlooking Playa de Burriana, a splendid establishment to crown the hotel list of Nerja.

Regarding tourist accommodation, perhaps the chief peculiarity of Nerja is the

Aerial view of part of the city.

large number of housing developments, evidence of the faithfulness of visitors choosing the area for their holidays. There are more than 60 of these developments spread over the municipality, the most famous of them being El Capistrano, which has the structure of an Andalusian village, combining this traditional concept with the most up-to-date leisure and entertainment facilities.

Nerja has a golf course and a camp site, both situated just off the N-340 Maro road. A short list of the amenities of this area would include the La Coladilla golf course, situated between Fuente del Badén and the Nerja Cave, the pleasure port, Puerto Europa, to the west of the municipality, a water theme park, a riding school and many more. The re-

cent opening of the Málaga-Nerja dual carriageway has provided further impulse to tourist development.

Nerja town centre has preserved the traditional style of the Andalusian village. Whilst in many tourist resorts economic development and changes made in order to accommodate the arrival of mass tourism, transforming the houses and streets of entire towns, almost always for the worse, Nerja has not only conserved its original structure, but all new constructions have been adapted to the traditional Andalusian style of whitewashed houses, windows with grilles, roofs with two slopes, etc.

Though its urban structure reflects Moorish influences, most of the town is of more recent construction, since in 1884 a major earthquake destroyed

Calahonda beach.

Dusk over the Balcón de Europa.

Promenade of the Balcón de Europa.

Hermitage of the Virgen de las Angustias. ▷

Burriana beach.

Beautiful view of the Balcón de Europa from Calahonda.

The Promenade.

*Fountain in
Plaza de Cantarero.*

*Some of the varied
landscapes around
the coastline of Nerja.*

The cliffs.

The ancient cannons of the fortress still watch over the coast from the Balcón de Europa.

Nerja, as well as devastating other villages in La Axarquía. Its main streets, long and winding, run down seemingly in search of the sea: Calle Cristo, Calle Pintada, Paseo Nuevo and Calle Granada.

The nerve centre of Nerja is the Balcón de Europa, a favourite site with local people and visitors alike. The promenade, flanked on the left by lovely arches and on the right by hotels, bars and restaurants, ends at a semi-circular viewpoint at the cliff-top, commanding magnificent views over the Mediterranean and the mountains around Nerja. Sunset seen from the Balcón de Europa is unforgettable. The promenade is lined with palms and plane trees, and two ancient cannons form a reminder that until 1812 there was a fortress at the top of the cliffs. At the opposite end to the viewpoint, turning left, is a square containing the Church of El Salvador.

Between the Calahonda and Carabeo beaches runs the Paseo de los Carabineros, a delightful natural pathway among the rocks of the coastline. Further east are the Jardines de Europa, charming botanic gardens which slope down to the Playa de Burriana.

The municipality also contains vestiges of prehistoric times: in the Nerja Cave, remains have been found from the Paleolithic period, some 30,000 years in the remote past. Neolithic, Copper, Bronze and Iron age artefacts have also been unearthed here, as well as much evidence of the Roman occupation. The Roman town of Detunda was located close to Maro, and burial places,

Long, languid Burriana beach.

pottery and coins have been found. Remains of the old Castulo-Malaca Roman road have also been discovered in the municipality. This road linked the provinces of Jaén and Almería, and from Nerja followed the coastline to the city of Málaga. Two stretches of this way have been identified, and the remains of a Roman bridge close to an old sugar mills just a few hundred metres from the site of El Capistrano residential area.

The origins of Nerja go back to Moorish times, when it was known variously as *Narixa, Naricha* or *Narija,* meaning, as we have mentioned, «abundant spring». The site of the town in those days was different, being rather more inland than that of present-day Nerja. Remains of the Moorish settlement have been found, together with vestiges of a fortress on the Frigiliana road. The Moors also built another castle on the coast, on the cliffs where we can now admire splendid views from the Balcón de Europa.

Narixa enjoyed great economic prosperity from the 10th century onwards, due to its agricultural and silk industries, products well-known in the markets of Damascus.

During this period, the town formed part of the *cora,* or province, of Rayya, to which Málaga also belonged. Nerja is mentioned by two 10th-century scholars, the historian Almacarri de Tremecen and the geographer Ibn Saadi, who dedicated some verses to this Moorish town, according to the modern historian Vázquez Otero:

El Capistrano seen from Burriana beach.

«Stretched out on magically-coloured carpets whilst sweet dreams my eyes closed, Naricha, my Naricha, springing up among flowers with all its beauties my sight delighted».

The town offered no resistance to the conquering Catholic Monarchs, who took the area in 1487, sparing the Morisca population.

During the 16th and 17th centuries, the population of Nerja was seriously diminished due to a number of dramatic events. The first was the Moorish uprising of 1568, the most far-reaching in effect the final expulsion of the Moors in 1609, after which the area was repopulated by what were known as «old Christians».

In 1509, the castle on the cliffs was rebuilt, and it was from this moment that the present site occupied by Nerja began to take shape, as the population began to construct houses and other buildings around this fortress and along the coast nearby. In 1571 another castle was constructed on the Torrecilla beach, completing the defensive system with that of the cliffs and the watchtowers of the area.

The 16th century marked the beginning of a period of economic prosperity with the introduction of sugar cane and the establishment of sugar mills in the area. In 1808, the Napoleonic invasion began, and Nerja also witnessed important episodes later, during the War of Independence. In 1812, the English fleet, allied to Spain, destroyed the Torrecilla and Balcón de Europa castles to prevent them from falling into French hands.

The hotels in the west of the city.

The late-19th century saw the occurrence of two unfortunate incidents here. The first began towards the end of 1875. A plague of phylloxera destroyed most of the vines in the district, causing an enormous economic disaster.

The second occurred on 25 December 1884. This was a large earthquake, which affected much of the provinces of Málaga and Granada. This destroyed

Sunshades in a tiny cove.

The tropical fruit plantations reach right down to the sea.

Apartments at Punta Lara.

A pool, El Capistrano. ▷

Various views of El Capistrano residential area.

Fishermen's house
on the rocks of the c[...]

A view of the
Promenade of the
Balcón de Europa.

«El Puente del Aguila», an ancient aqueduct.

much of the town, though there was only one mortal victim, a Carabinero called Berrocal. Due to the magnitude of the disaster, King Alfonso XII visited the area, arriving in Nerja on 20 January 1885, accompanied by his ministers, Quesada and Romero Robledo. After inspecting the devastated streets of the town, it is said that the ruler was so struck by the beauty of the view from the end of the promenade that he himself suggested the world-famous title of «Balcón de Europa» («Balcony of Europe») for it, though in reality it was already known by that name.

Let us now take a short tour of the monuments of Nerja, beginning with the Almenar towers. These are watchtowers built to protect the area against

Tourists sunbathing by the fishing boats in a cove around Nerja.

NERJA

A FRIGILIANA 6 KM.

A MALAGA 52 KM.

N- 340

CARRETERA

RIO CHILLAR

Rambla Río Chillar

Chaparil

Las Terrazas

Pérez

Plaza de la Marina

Jaén

Ebn Sad

Manuel Marín

Antonio

Millón

Castilla

Diputación Provincia

Chaparil

Fray Junipero Serra

Avenida

El Barrio

Málaga

Avenida

Almirante Carranza

Dr. Fle mming

Mediterráneo

Pedro de Valdivia

Doctor Ferrán

Mérida

Torrecilla

Nuñez de Balboa

Hernán Cortés

Pizarro

Málaga

Mirador

PLAYA DEL PLAYAZO

PLAYA DEL SAL

PLAYA DE LA TORRECILLA

MA

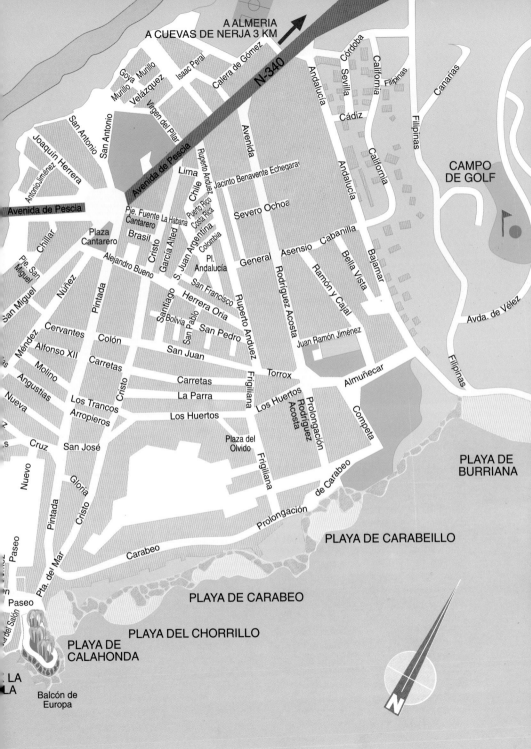

A ALMERIA
A CUEVAS DE NERJA 3 KM

N-340

Goya
Murillo
Murillo
Velázquez
Isaac Peral
Calera de Gómez
Córdoba
Sevilla
California
Filipinas
Canarias
Andalucía
Cádiz
Filipinas
San Antonio
San Antonio
Virgen del Pilar
Avenida
California
CAMPO
DE GOLF
Joaquín Herrera
Antonio Jiménez Herrera
Avenida de Pescia
Lima
Ruperto Andúez
Jacinto Benavente
Echegaray
Chile
Andalucía
Avenida de Pescia
Pje. Fuente La Habana
Cantarero
Puerto Rico
Costa Rica
Severo Ochoa
Plaza
Cantarero
Brasil
Cristo
García Aled
S. Juan Argentina
Colombia
Colombia
General
Asensio
Cabanilla
Bajamar
Avda. de Vélez
Chillar
Alejandro Bueno
Pl.
Andalucía
San Francisco
Ruperto Andúez
Rodríguez Acosta
Ramón y Cajal
Bella Vista
Pje. San
Miguel
Núñez
Pintada
Santiago
Herrera Oria
Bolivia
San Pablo
San Pedro
Juan Ramón Jiménez
Filipinas
San Miguel
Cervantes
Colón
San Juan
Torrox
Almuñecar
Mendez
Alfonso XII
Carretas
Cristo
Frigiliana
Los Huertos
Prolongación
Rodríguez
Acosta
Cómpeta
Molino
Carretas
La Parra
PLAYA DE
BURRIANA
Angustias
Los Trancos
Los Huertos
Nueva
Arropieros
Nuevo
San José
Plaza del
Olvido
Frigiliana
Prolongación
de Carabeo
PLAYA DE CARABEILLO
Gloria
Pintada
Cristo
Paseo
Pta. del Mar
Carabeo
PLAYA DE CARABEO
Paseo
del Salón
PLAYA DEL CHORRILLO
LA
LA
PLAYA DE
CALAHONDA
Balcón de
Europa

N

MEDITERRANEO

The golf course next to El Capistrano.

Many of the streets of Nerja overlook the sea. ▷

the attacks of pirates from the African coast. Acting as beacons, they would light warning fires which carried the alarm from one to the next at any sign of danger. There were five such towers along the Nerja coastline, from west to east: Torrecilla, Torre de Maro, Torre del Río de la Miel, Torre del Pino and Torre de Cañuelo. Some are of Nazarí-Moorish origin, whilst others were built after the Christian reconquest.

There are three churches in the town of Nerja. The Church of El Salvador was built in 1697, though it was altered and extended at the end of the 18th century and has recently been restored. It is built in a Baroque-Mudéjar style, and its interior contains a nave and two aisles, the nave covered by a Mudéjar coffered ceiling. There is a splendid mural by Francisco Hernández. The tower, ad-

joining the simple front, has a square groundplan, though the upper section, containing the bell, is octagonal.

The Baroque Hermitage of the Virgen de las Angustias was built in 1720. Inside there is a single nave, with interesting al fresco paintings in the vault. These are 18th-century works of the Granada school by Alonso Cano, representing Pentecost and the Four Evangelists. The exterior of this hermitage features a tiny atrium supported by four pillars.

The Church of San Miguel was built in much more recent times (1977).

Between Nerja and Maro, visible from the N-340 road, is the Aguila Aqueduct, built in the 19th century over the Barranco de Maro and used for transporting water to the Maro Sugar Factory. It consists of five storeys of super-

An aerial view of the city.

◁ *The Paseo de Europa.*

«The Rape of Europe», a fine sculpture in bronze standing at the entrance to Nerja.

A seaside view with, in the background, «The Rape of Europe».

Coves and cliffs, a constant feature of Nerja.

An ancient cannon on the Balcón de Europa.

Tropical fruits are grown widely in the region.

Nerja lies between the sea and the mountains.

posed brick arches and was designed by the Nerja-born architect Francisco Cantarero.

At the entrance to the town is a bronze sculpture representing the mythological theme of the rape of Europa.

We will complete our tour of the monuments of Nerja with what has become known, due to its incomparable beauty and historic importance, as the Natural Prehistoric Cathedral: the Nerja Cave. The cave was discovered by five young people from Maro in January 1959, and was opened to the public the following year. At the entrance, a monument by the sculptor Carlos Monteverde commemorates the discovery of the cave.

To get to the cave, take the N-340 Granada road to a turn-off shortly before Maro. The site lies at 700 metres from the coast, in the dying foothills of the Sierra Almijara. Underground streams perforated the limestone of these mountains, forming huge chambers and strange and lovely stalactites and stalagmites.

The cave was inhabited as far back as the Higher Paleolithc Age, 30,000 years ago. Remains of Cro-Magnon man have been found here, as well as artefacts from the Solutrian Age. It was used during the Neolithic and Chalcolithic ages, and ceased to be inhabited around 3,000 years ago.

Salón beach.

The cave consists of two sections: the zone open to the public, around one kilometre in length, and the parts not open to visitors, around double the length of the former. In this part, sound and light equipment has been installed to improve access and make the visit more interesting.

The first two chambers are the Sala de Belén («the crib») and the Sala del Colmillo de Elefante («elephant's tusk»). Next is the Sala de la Cascada («water-fall»). This chamber is 30 metres high and has been converted into an original setting for the internationally famous Festival of Dance and Music, held every summer since 1960 in this chamber, which seat some 800 spectators.

The visit continues with the Sala de los Fantasmas («ghosts») and that of El Cataclismo, in whose centre there is a column formed by the fusion of a sta-lactite and a stalagmite, with a diameter of 18 metres.

The chambers which cannot be visited, some of them spectacularly beautiful, are: the Sala de las Columnas de Hércules («the Columns of Hercules»), the Sala de la Inmensidad («immen-sity»), the Sala de los Niveles («levels»), the Sala de la Lanza («the spear») and the Sala de la Montaña («the moun-tain»).

The walls of the Nerja Cave are covered with interesting cave paintings, out-standing of which are the *Capra Hispánica* in the Sala de los Fantasmas and the Red Deer in that of El Cataclismo.

The importance of the Nerja Cave has caused it to be declared a Historic and Artistic Monument. Much of the attrac-tion of Nerja for tourists is, without doubt, due to this natural marvel.

Church of San Salvador, a Baroque building dating back to the 17th century.

At the cave entrance is a small archaeological museum displaying some of the objects discovered inside. Outside, the visitor will find a restaurant, café and other facilities. Nerja stages a wide variety of cultural and festive activities, beginning the year with Carnival, a tradition which has recently been recovered. At Easter, several *pasos* (floats) lead processions through the streets of the town. Holy Week is celebrated here with great emotion and simplicity. The festivity of 3 May is also important in Nerja, and two specialities are prepared for this day, *arropía* and *marcocha,* both made with honey. On 15 May, the Romería de San Isidro takes place, a pilgrimage involving gaily-decorated carts and horses. The lavishness here of the commemorations for the patron saint of farming is a clear sign of the importance of agriculture in the economy of Nerja. Another outstanding festivity is 24 June, Saint John's day. The tradition on this day is to go down to the beach to enjoy the speciality of the feast, *torta de San Juan.* The importance of the sea for Nerja is reflected in the feasts in honour of the Virgen del Carmen, on 16 July. A statue of this virgin is carried through the streets of the town before begin taken on board a boat and paraded along the coastline. The day's festivities include regattas, sports competitions and the consumption of grilled sardines on the beach. Nerja Fair takes place from 9-13 October in honour of the patron saints of the town, Michael and the Virgen de las Angustias. Regarding strictly cultural events, there are two outstanding occasions to mention: the International Music Week and the Festival of Dance and Music, held every year in Nerja Cave.

An overall view of Maro.

Cala de Maro. ▷

MARO

Three kilometres from Nerja, along the N-340 Granada road, is the tiny village of Maro, which belongs to the municipality of Nerja. It has a population of some 800.

The fields and gardens of Maro stretch down almost to the sea, in terraces sloping down the sides of the mountains.

Every summer, thousands of visitors flock to Maro to relax in the charming coves of its coastline. To cope with this tourist trade, a great many bars, restaurants and hotels have opened in recent years, whilst there is also a camp site nearby.

The Nerja Cave is very close to the village, as are the ruins of the ancient Roman city of Detunda. The main monument in Maro is its Church of Nuestra Señora de las Maravillas, building of which began in the early-17th century, though due to the devastation caused by the earthquake in 1884, it was restored at the end of the 19th century. Inside, there is a single nave with a wooden ceiling. The exterior of the church is simple, with a square tower adjoining the front.

The Maro Sugar Factor, or sugar mill, was built in the 17th century and reformed in the 19th, when the industry was at its peak of prosperity.

The annual festivities of Maro commence on 17 January, Saint Anthony's day. The occasion is celebrated with firework displays and a procession led by the statue of the saint. On 9 September, the Feria de las Maravillas is held in honour of the patron saint of the village.

Church of Nuestra Señora de las Maravillas.

The Cave entrance.

An interior view of Nerja Cave. ▷

Overall view of Frigiliana.

Partial view of Frigiliana. ▷

FRIGILIANA

The environs of Nerja contain a number of highly interesting localities and beauty spots which will delight the tourist. The nearby villages form part of the Sun and Wine Route, which takes in the municipalities of Algarrobo, Sayalonga, Cómpeta, Canillas de Albaida, Torrox, Frigiliana and Nerja. The route takes its name from the fact that, as well as important tourist resorts such as Nerja, Torrox or Algarrobo, it includes inland villages which produce excellent wine. The streets and squares of these attractive villages retain a clearly Moorish air.

The closest of these villages to Nerja is Frigiliana. On leaving the town, take the Málaga road, where a turn-off leads the six kilometres to this lovely spot.

The municipal area of Frigiliana borders with Cómpeta to the north, Torrox to the west and with Nerja to the east and south. The district, irrigated by the Higuerón, a tributary of the Chillar, grows sub-tropical fruits and vegetables. The dry-farming areas cultivate basically olives and grapes, from which excellent wines, both sweet and dry, are made. The road to Frigiliana is flanked by a large number of residential areas, occupied mostly by Central Europeans. The village centre, at an altitude of 435 metres above sea level, lies in the Sierra de Enmedio, the southern section of the Sierra Almijara. Frigiliana has a population of over 2,000, and is 56 kilometres from Málaga.

Frigiliana consists of two adjoining centres of population. One of these is ancient, of Moorish origin, and the other

"Andrés el Chorairán monfí natural de Sedella, conci-
tó los ánimos de los suyos para escitarles a la rebelión. La gente moza que comenzaba a alborotarse la
contuvo el morisco Luis Mendez, hombre influyente
en Canillas, pero no pudo evitar que atacaran una
venta de un cristiano, ni que mataran en ella a varias
personas. Acudió el Juez de Vélez Pedro Gue-
rra, y muchos inocentes moriscos, entre ellos Luis
Mendez, que había impedido la revuelta, fueron
presos y cargados de cadenas, y sometidos a crue-
les tormentos."

Guillen Robles. 'Historia de Málaga y su provincia' Cap. XV, Málaga, 1873.

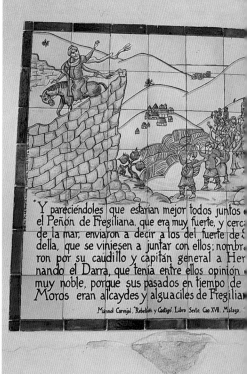

"Y pareciéndoles que estarían mejor todos juntos
el Peñón de Fregiliana, que era muy fuerte, y cerca
de la mar, enviaron a decir a los del fuerte de S
della, que se viniesen a juntar con ellos; nombr.
ron por su caudillo y capitán general a Her
nando el Darra, que tenía entre ellos opinión
muy noble, porque sus pasados en tiempo de
Moros eran alcaydes y alguaciles de Fregilia

Manuel Carvajal, 'Rebelión y Castigo', Libro Sexto, Cap. XVII, Málaga.

Some of the streets of Frigiliana are decorated with mosaics which recount episodes of the history of the town.

A typical Moorish street. ▷

much more recently built, but retaining the structure of a typical Andalusian village. Between these two districts are two interesting buildings: the former Pósito (granary), built in 1767, and a 16th-century Renaissance mansion, the Palacio de los Montijanos, now converted into a molasses factory.

The Moorish village is one of the best-preserved in the entire province of Málaga, or even of Andalusia. For this reason, Frigiliana has received many prizes for its beauty and excellent conservation. Its narrow, steeply-winding stony streets perfectly retain their original Moorish flavour. One of the most attractive features of Frigiliana is the vast abundance of plants and flowers which adorn the whitewashed streets of this Malagan village.

During the course of our tour around the streets of the Moorish quarter, we can admire a number of ceramic panels, designed by Pilar García Millán and made by Amparo Ruiz de Luna, which add a further decorative touch to the village and, at the same time, narrate the story of the Moorish uprising here. Though the most notable episode in the history of Frigiliana was the Moorish uprising, settlement here goes back to prehistoric times, and sites going back to between 3000 and 1500 BC have been discovered nearby, as well as Phoenician remains in the Cerrillo de las Sombras, dating back to the 7th and 6th centuries BC, and evidence of the Roman occupation of these lands.

Frigiliana enjoyed great importance during Moorish times, when a castle was built at the highest point in the village and whose ruins may still be seen.

Molasses factory.

Church of San Antonio. ▷

In 1487, Frigiliana was conquered by the Catholic Monarchs, and from that time on its Moorish population lived under constant pressure. The resentment caused led to the outbreak of the Moorish uprisings in 1569, not just here but in the entire district of La Axarquía and the adjoining Alpujarra region. One of the main battles during this rebellion was fought in Frigiliana on 11 June 1569, the rebels from both districts having joined together on the heights of the village under the command of El Darra. Both rebels and official troops suffered heavy losses.

In 1609, the defeated Moors were expelled from Spain to North Africa. The castle of Frigiliana was almost completely destroyed.

The Moorish quarter is crossed lengthways by the main street of the village. At the top of Frigiliana, this street opens out into a square containing the Church of San Antonio, built in the 16th century. The most outstanding feature of the exterior of this building is its clocktower, whilst the interior has a fine choir, silver treasures in the sacristy and three 17th-century paintings. The church has a nave and two aisles, with Mudéjar coffered ceilings.

Finally, there are two interesting hermitages here. These are the Hermitage of San Sebastián, at the edge of the village, and that of Ecce Homo, in the new district.

Regarding local festivities, on 20 January is the Feast of Saint Sebastian, and

Partial view of the village.

A typical street. ▷

on May 3 the streets of Frigiliana are adorned with crosses. Lastly, from 11-14 June, around the Feast of Saint Anthony, the Battle of the Peñón de Frigiliana is commemorated by the Romería of Las Lomas de las Vacas.

Another locality pertaining to the Sun and Wine Route is Algarrobo. The town centre of this municipality is four kilometres inland, 20 kilometres from Nerja. It has a stable population of 4,500, greatly increased during the summer months by the arrival of tourists visiting the coast, as the resorts of Mezquitilla and Algarrobo-Costa have become very popular.

The most important monuments in Algarrobo are the Hermitage of San Sebastián, a modern construction, and the Church of Santa Ana, which dates back to the 18th century. At various places in the district are Bronze Age sites, as well as evidence of Phoenician, Carthaginian and Roman occupation. The most interesting of these are those at Chorreras and Trayamar. The festivities for the patron saint of Algarrobo are held on 20 January, Saint Sebastian's day, and a fair is held here every summer.

Sayalonga is another village on the Sun and Wine Route, and is six kilometres from Algarrobo. This is a picturesque village with a population of 1,300, situated at an altitude of 350 metres above sea level.

The village has two churches: The Church of Santa Catalina, built in the

Flowers frequently adorn the houses of the region.

16th century, and the Chapel of San Antón. There is an interesting cemetery.

The main festivities here are: 7 October (day of the patron saint, the Virgen del Rosario) 15 August and 7-8 September (Candelmass).

Overall view of Cómpeta.

Fountain in Plaza Almijara, Cómpeta. ▷

COMPETA

This is one of the most interesting villages of the district. There are two ways of reaching Cómpeta, which is 27 kilometres from Nerja: continuing along the same road after leaving Sayalonga for another nine kilometres, or through Torrox.

Cómpeta lies on the southern slopes of the Sierra Almijara, at a height of 650 metres above sea level. The municipal area contains a large number of springs and streams which bring down water from the surrounding mountains. The district contains many peaks, including El Cisne, Cerro Verde and Cerro Lucero. Due to its situation close to the Tejeda and Almijara sierras, Cómpeta is the starting-point for excursions and hikers.

The main agricultural product of the area is the grape, and the wineries of Cómpeta are famed for producing one of the finest wines of Málaga.

The urban layout of the village is typically Moorish. From the main square – Plaza de Almijara – picturesquely beautiful streets fan out, flanked by whitewashed houses and adorned with flowers and plants.

Plaza de Almijara is the site of the Church of La Asunción, built towards the end of the 16th century in Baroque-Mudéjar style. Its finest feature is the ochre-coloured tower, of late-19th-century construction, though finally completed in 1935. This is in Neo-Mudéjar style, adorned with brickwork and mosaics. The beauty and stylised forms of this tower make it stand out from the

Two typical nooks in La Axarquía.

rest in La Axarquía. Cómpeta also contains two hermitages: that of San Antón, dating back to the 18th century, and that of San Sebastián.

Particularly because of its name, Cómpeta is thought to be Roman in origin, though no definitive evidence of this has been found. The village enjoyed a certain splendour during the times of the Moorish domination due to its thriving agricultural industry, and fell into Christian hands along with the rest of the district in 1487. Cómpeta played an important role in the Moorish uprisings, whose centre was the Alpujarra district, in the 16th century. In this district, the leader was Martín Alwacin who, at the beginning had remained neutral being forced by the pressure of the Moorish population to place himself at the head of the rebels. At first, the Moors enjoyed a number of military successes, but were finally defeated in 1569 in a battle near Frigiliana. The Moorish population was expelled from these lands during the early part of the following century.

The main festivities in Cómpeta take place from 22-25 June, in honour of Saint Sebastian, the patron saint. Other important occasions are the «Day of the Cross» on 3 May, 7-8 September (Day of La Virgen) and, above all, the «Noche del Vino» (Night of Wine) on 15 August, when thousands of visitors descend on Cómpeta to taste the excellent wine of the district.

From Cómpeta it is just three kilometres to another interesting village, Canillas de Albaida. This tiny village, whose layout is typically Moorish, has a population of 700. The main square

Lighthouse at Punta de Torrox.

contains the Church of Nuestra Señora de la Expectación, constructed during the 16th and 17th centuries. Its outstanding feature is the tower, built of stone and brick. Other monuments are the 16th-century Hermitage of Santa Ana, and the 17th-century Hermitage of San Antón. Festivities include the feast of Saint Anton on 17 January and the Virgin of the Rosary (7 October).

TORROX

Torrox is situated 12 kilometres from Nerja and is one of the most important towns in La Axarquía, its municipal area

The broad beaches of Torrox-Costa.

Torrox-Costa: the sea front.

containing a stretch of coastline which includes the tourist resorts of El Morche and Torrox-Costa. Not including summer residents and visitors, the population of Torrox stands at around 12,000. Settlement around Torrox goes back to the Phoenician colonisation, but the most important archaeological site here is the Roman town at El Faro, known as Clavicum. This settlement dates back to the 1st-4th centuries. There are Roman baths, ovens, the remains of dwellings and troughs used for making garum (a type of fish paste).

Torrox was also settled by the Moors, who built a castle at the highest point of the village.

Like Nerja, Torrox prospered greatly under the Moors due to its agricultural produce and silk industry. It is said, though proof has not been found, that the famous Caliph Almanzor was born in Torrox. The earthquake of 1884 also caused great damage here, and King Alfonso XII stayed in Torrox during his visit to the disaster zone.

The monuments of Torrox include the Church of Nuestra Señora de la Encarnación, a Mudéjar building which dates back to the 17th century. Other important monuments are: The Hermitage and Convent of Nuestra Señora de las Nieves, a 16th-century construction, the Hermitage of San Roque, the 18th-century Hospital of San José and the Sugar Factory.

Regarding festivities, the most unusual is the Fiesta de las Migas, held on the Sunday before Christmas. During this feast, local wine is drunk, accompanied by the local gastronomic speciality, *migas* (fried breadcrumbs).

Fried fish and anchovies.

Grilled sardines.

GASTRONOMY

The *cuisine* of Nerja has much in common with that of La Axarquía and Málaga. The principal base of local cooking is olive oil, produced in the districts around Nerja and of excellent quality. Nevertheless, Nerja has its own specialities, especially as regards desserts, the main reason for the existence of this section of the book. It will be seen that most of the characteristics of local dishes are taken from traditional Moorish cooking.

A typical dish is *gazpacho,* whether cold, in varieties such as *zoque* or *ajoblanco,* or hot, such as *gazpachuelo.* All the restaurants and «chiringuitos» of Nerja specialise in *pescaíto frito,* fried fish, most typically anchovies, squid and red mullet.

◁ *Panda de Verdiales.*

Migas (fried breadcrumbs) another popular dish in La Axarquía.

The popular dish Cazuela de Choto.

Typical gazpacho andaluz.

Another popular fish here are sardines, eaten from *espetos,* skewers, often grilled on the beach.

Typical main dishes are *migas* and *choto* (kid). The latter can be eaten fried, *al ajillo* (baked in garlic) or with an almond sauce. *Choto* is a speciality of Frigiliana, whilst another typical dish from Nerja is *pimentón.*

Regarding desserts, honey and batatas form the most delicious basis of the local specialities. The most typical is a combination of the two, *batatas con miel,* consisting of the tasty local batatas cooked in molasses.

During the festivities of the Cruces de Mayo, two other desserts are made using honey: *arropía,* sweets, and *marcocha,* popcorn covered in honey. For the Feast of Saint John, delicious *tortas de San Juan* are made.

Lastly, we should make special mention of the wines made from the grapes grown around Nerja. Most of the DOC wines of Málaga are produced in the vineyards of this area and of La Axarquía in general. Though various types of dry wines exist, the best-known internationally are the sweet wines, and in particular Pedro Ximénez, lágrima and moscatel. The wines of Cómpeta and Frigiliana are especially recommended.

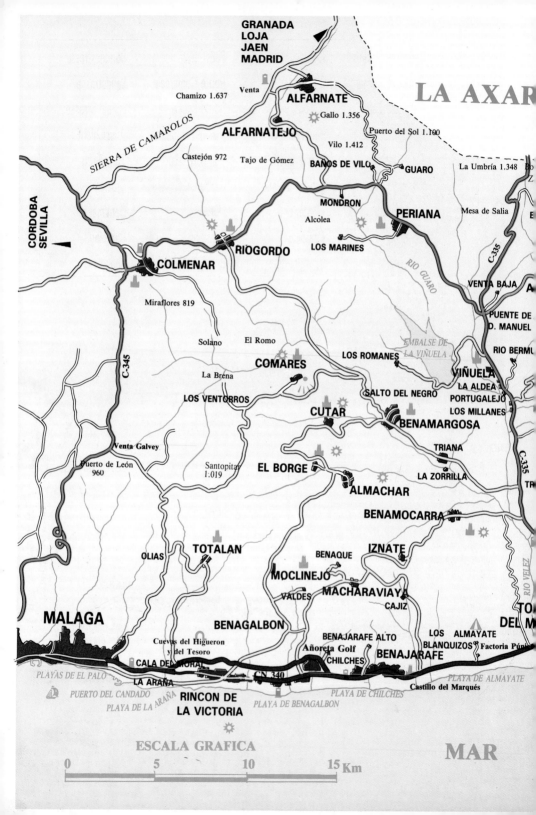

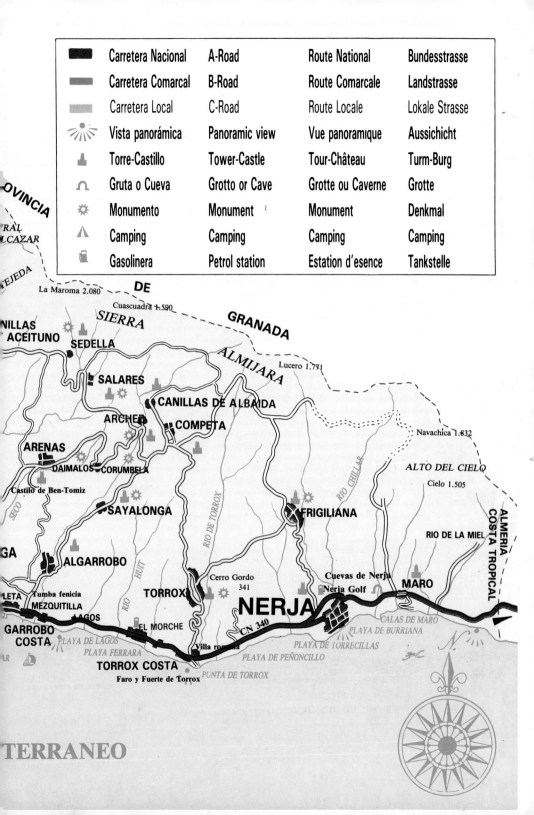

	Carretera Nacional	A-Road	Route National	Bundesstrasse
	Carretera Comarcal	B-Road	Route Comarcale	Landstrasse
	Carretera Local	C-Road	Route Locale	Lokale Strasse
	Vista panorámica	Panoramic view	Vue panoramique	Aussichicht
	Torre-Castillo	Tower-Castle	Tour-Château	Turm-Burg
	Gruta o Cueva	Grotto or Cave	Grotte ou Caverne	Grotte
	Monumento	Monument	Monument	Denkmal
	Camping	Camping	Camping	Camping
	Gasolinera	Petrol station	Estation d'esence	Tankstelle

OVINCIA
RAL
LCAZAR
EJEDA

La Maroma 2.080
DE
Cuascuadra 1.590
SIERRA
GRANADA
NILLAS
ACEITUNO
SEDELLA
ALMIJARA
Lucero 1.731
SALARES
CANILLAS DE ALBAIDA
ARCHE
COMPETA
Navachica 1.832
ARENAS
DAIMALOS CORUMBELA
ALTO DEL CIELO
Cielo 1.505
Castilo de Ben-Tomiz
SAYALONGA
RIO CHILLAR
FRIGILIANA
RIO DE LA MIEL
GA
ALGARROBO
ALMERIA COSTA TROPICAL
LETA
Tumba fenicia
MEZQUITILLA
Cerro Gordo
341
Cuevas de Nerja
Nerja Golf
MARO
TORROX
NERJA
LAGOS
CALAS DE MARO
GARROBO
COSTA
EL MORCHE
PLAYA DE LAGOS
CN 340
PLAYA DE BURRIANA
PLAYA FERRARA
Villa romana
PLAYA DE TORRECILLAS
N.
TORROX COSTA
PLAYA DE PEÑONCILLO
Faro y Fuerte de Torrox
PUNTA DE TORROX

TERRANEO

The printing of this book was completed
in the workshops of
FISA - ESCUDO DE ORO, S.A.
Palaudarias, 26 - Barcelona (Spain)